THE GO-AWAY BIRD

ALSO BY SENI SENEVIRATNE

Wild Cinnamon and Winter Skin
The Heart of It
Unknown Soldier

SENI SENEVIRATNE

THE GO-AWAY BIRD

PEEPAL TREE

First published in Great Britain in 2023
Peepal Tree Press Ltd
17 King's Avenue
Leeds LS6 1QS
UK

ISBN: 9781845235567

Printed in the United Kingdom
by Severn, Gloucester,
on responsibly sourced paper

MIX
Paper from
responsible sources
FSC® C022174

Supported by
ARTS COUNCIL
ENGLAND

CONTENTS

FOR THE BIRDS

CHOOK, WHEET, SIP, TITIT, CHIRP, TWITTER, KEKKEKKEK,

coo-ree, seep-ep, reekareeka,
warble, siff siff siff, chiff chaff –
every attempt to suggest a word
for the sound of a bird is bound
to fall short and end up merely
as guessed-at random translations
of a language that is so far removed
from the tongue of the human species –
chatter, chup, chirrup, croak, shek shek,
shriek, growl, twe twe, trill, chichichi ……

by which I mean discovery of the particular location of the syrinx, known commonly as one of the two voice boxes that every bird possesses, although the one more familiarly named larynx doesn't make any sound at all in the species, it is not surprising, given the way the sounding syrinx sits so snugly at the base of their windpipe and so close to their heart, that the calls of birds which are numerous and difficult to translate accurately into human word forms, carry a breath and beat that reaches my ear and body simultaneously in a kind of heart-hearing that pushes a silent sigh up and out of me.

THAT'S FOR THE BIRDS

I was the youngest of three, with scuffed knees
mucky after playing-out adventures in our garden

where my sister and I were always the Indians
running from a gun-slinging cowboy brother

to hide in bushes where sparrows made untidy nests.
Later, still grubby from the day's play, I'd watch

through the window, hear their chirruping tetetetete
as they gathered to peck our offerings on the lawn.

"That's for the birds", my mum would say, chopping
bacon rind and scooping bread crumbs into a bowl.

I was a little brown girl, nose pressed up to the glass,
watching little brown birds roll around in the dust.

A BIT OF COAL

And then there were my grandma's pet budgies –
first Joey then Peter or was it Peter then Joey?

What I do recall is one or other caged bird
in the alcove next to the blackened fire range

very close to the door and the steps leading
down into the dark unknown of the cellar.

"We need a bit of coal," she'd say, "for the fire."
Then that fearful walk – past the blue of Joey

or the green of Peter with one thought: I'd rather
take your place, be a caged bird, if it saved me from

the unseen four-legged creatures that lurked below
and the sound of their scuttling as I rattled the bucket.

PICKING A CHICKEN

I never thought of the bird as something
that was once alive. The picking was a ritual,

something special between me and my grandma,
an invitation to her scullery kitchen, a space made

for the unfinished carcass amidst all the aftermath
of cooking, a time for my small fingers to pick

at the scraps of meat between the bones, for sucking
and savouring the leftovers, for saving the wishbone

to dry and pull. It was nothing about a bird.
It was family, sustenance and being the chosen one.

MYTHS AND MAGIC

Pliny was witness to the days when chickens, kept
as auspices, foretold the victories of ancient Rome.

Aristotle, too, upheld the old belief that nightjars
stole the milk of goats by sucking on their teats.

And one archaic name for swifts was devil birds
as if their screaming cries were harbingers of hell.

More recently my grandma harboured fears of peacocks,
warned me to be wary of the eye-spots on their tails.

IF EVER

I'm not sure if they ever happened,
the fearful conversations across the gap
between our beds, willing it to stay alive
until the morning so we could collect
more earthworms and carry water
in tiny teacups to drip feed, looking for
some small sign of recovery in the shoebox
lined with soft things our mum had helped us find
after she'd put aside her worries about the germs
a wounded bird might harbour since the sight
of our sparrow's lolling broken wing had melted
her resolve, even though she would have said,
"It's not a creature meant to be indoors", which is why
it would have stayed in our Dream House shed
where we had first hidden it because it was a secret
and my sister would have been in on it
if ever I found an injured bird as a child.

AND WOULD I HAVE LOVED TO FLY?

Lift off above the semi-detached houses on our road
from the tiled roof above the stained-glass windows,

soar with unfamiliar ease up, up to meet a multitude
of starlings. That day there'd be no heavy satchel,

no hunched shoulders under a duffel coat, no long walk
through the housing estate alone on my way to school.

Only the whoosh of my wings like a great black cape,
the calls of my fellow travellers weaving in and out,

"No school this morning, we're out to play, painting
the sky with black swirls in our startling composition."

ADOLESCENT BIRD

I always come back
to the same tight patch of grass

but I'm kicking my heels
waiting for the off again;

can't sleep at night
for the wings knocking

at my window pane
the other side of the curtains.

The world's a rough ride
however high you fly

but when I'm up there
with the blackest birds I can find,

though buffeted and windswept,
I can look down to see how the land lies.

BREATHING IN

That morning I caught the particular scent
of another Spring on its way and with it
a sense of being a being at any age, in any year
of my life so far, all at once. Not so much
timeless as timefull: full to bursting with times
past and present all held together by
the familiarity of breathing in a new season.
Forever a creature in wellies and a warm coat,
stepping outdoors to welcome the first swallows.

LOCKDOWN AT LEIGHTON MOSS

One day later, there'd have been no young woman
with purple hair greeting us in the visitor centre,
telling us how the booming bitterns could be heard
somewhere along the lower trail past Lilian's Hide.
Nervous at the sight of a man touching his face
while he stacks the coffee cups, we escape outdoors
to walk between the reed beds, bask in the wide open
as everything else is closing down. Out of the expanse

comes the low moan of the bittern's call. It echoes from
untraceable directions, lands in the pivot of my pelvis,
my centre of gravity, a grounding place amidst shifting
uncertainties. Soon enough this place will be off-limits.
But today, lost in the thrill of the bittern's mating song,
I raise my binoculars and watch a marsh harrier soar.

MY LIGHT-BONED LOVER

has taken to carving corvids; the numbers
are growing. If we pass them in fields
she stops the car suddenly, waiting for take-off.

She spends hours studying their form,
shoulders hunched, smearing bold lines
of charcoal over page after page.

She says it's her wings, when her back
is aching, won't take the tablets the hospital
sent to strengthen her hollow bones.

Yesterday, I caught her gazing longingly
at their silhouettes in the trees on the horizon.
I know it's only a matter of time.

NIGHT CALLS

Somewhere out there beyond the open skylight, in our garden's night hours
from near distance
beyond the stream
there comes
an owl's cry
I inhale the sound and the waiting silence between, in the sleepless dark
not afraid
so much but
contemplating fear
and the way
it finds whatever resting place it can to land, to grow, to keep on shrieking.

LONG-TAILED TITS

Family birds at heart, they help out relatives
in a kind of extended communal roosting –
your own nest fails, so you find your kin.

I'm thinking about ruptures – close families
sometimes breaking open and how the gap
gets wider until it seems too far to cross.

And how I'm standing in the ever-growing
fracture, calling out like the long-tailed tits
to keep the conversation going because

my sisters, too far away from each other to hear
or be heard, may yet freeze without the huddle
as winter descends and no hope of a thaw.

What would mum and dad, if they were alive,
have to say? We never lost touch in our family
whatever happened. We're meant to stick together

like these tits, the black and white of them,
the smattering of grey and pink, marked out
by long narrow tails and short stubby bills.

We can't wait for Spring. Warmth comes
from sticking close and there's no such thing
as never when it comes to a family like ours.

Let's build nests of lichen, cobwebs, feathers.
There's enough danger from the elements
without harbouring harm inside the flock.

WINTER SOLSTICE

What is a fence after all but a definition of territory,
a declaration of ownership, a keep out, this-is mine,
no-go and all the more when not benign: not wood,
not hedge, not stone, not even wire alone but barbed.

And here it is, on this morning after snow, stopping me
in my tracks. The pity of it! The shame! The sight of
a hanging buzzard, a predator become prey, felled
with such ignominy by the winding of wire round wire.

No more soar and glide, no more hover and swoop,
only a drooping head, a lifeless claw clasping the wire,
one wing caught fast, the other reaching for the earth.

Oh mighty buzzard, how long was it before you ceased
to flail, before you were defeated? What ritual will suffice
to cleanse this place, still so heavy with your distress?

PHILOMELA REIMAGINED

PHILOMELA REIMAGINED

I'll shed my shame
And shout what you have done. If I've the chance,
I'll walk among the crowds: or if I'm held
Locked in the woods, my voice shall fill the woods
And move the rocks to pity...

(Ovid's Metamorphoses, Book VI –
translated A.D. Melville, Oxford University Pres

Philomela
time shattered   memory shot to pieces
a head full of 'if onlys'   his knife on my tongue
my beauty accused for the crime
speechless   unspeakable until
a certain kind of listening...

Tiresias
they say I'm a good listener
with stone-blind eyes that bless me with a second sight
though some days it feels like more of a curse than blessing
hard to keep my balance on this tightrope
above a faltering world

to read the sky's omens,
to follow the wisdom of birds
is a precarious path between vision and madness
but I'm used to walking through fire and ruin
and there's more than two sides to any story

I should know, I've tasted both sides
of a gendered life, didn't rest easy in either place
there's comfort in a certain kind of metamorphosis.

Philomela

Night after night his hollow bones stalk
my dreams like a death mask. He's all talk,
all promises and bunches of dead roses,
telling me I can trust him like family. And
I can never remember why I shouldn't.
He's bloody in the flame's trick of light,
but I'm the one in pieces with no time
to run before the candle's snuffed out.

I remember that I left. Like leaving
wounded bodies behind on a battlefield.
I was up in the trees, looking down
on the slaughter. And it was my body
down there, mauled by the enemy, mouth
open as if calling and calling. Though
in my ears there was only a cacophony
of birdsong that would not be silenced.

Were there signs I should have read,
omens I ignored? The trees mock me.
Their leaves, falling like silent tongues
turn to mulch on the forest floor.
I count for nothing. I see reflections
of myself in the cracked mirrors that hide
in their bark replaying my shame. I should
have done better, trusted less, run faster.

Felled trees are monuments to my demise,
their twisted limbs kick the air, as mine did.
I was nothing but dead wood, stripped bark
and pinned like his trophy to the forest floor.
What use is beauty without respect? What use
is kinship without trust? I'd rather be half-bird,
half-woman than prey to the fangs of wild men.
The rain dilutes everything. I am disappearing.

Tiresias

the crack of bark, some repeated action above guttural murmuring
breathing that tells me how hard she works
I know she feels threatened
by the way she moves to the space I have left
the way her breath quickens as she catches my arm
with a whip of young birch

Philomela

I gave up on humanity,
looked for succour in the language of birds,
in their comings and goings to a nest in the trees.

I watched how they gathered
the smallest things. How their weaving made circles.
I began to see how one stem could fit with another,

each fibre a memory in its proper place
and this damaged self learned how to build, learned
the uses of a beak. I was a creature among creatures

beginning to know the stillness of forest ways.
No judgement, no shame and water, like a sanctuary
was always running, always knew where it was going.

I gathered birchwood branches,
like time in no particular order, from the chaos
of bark, tied each one piece by piece. It took patience.

This easing of curved bark, this tying
and retying, over and over is how
I loved myself again, reordering the tricks

of time, conjuring survival. Some days,
I was tempted to make fire, burn everything
and disappear forever, surrendering

to a stolen future. But hope was another kind
of flame. In daylight, I considered the uses
of vengeance. At night, I fell exhausted

into nightmares but my own feathered nest
was waiting each morning, just as I had left it,
something to take hold of, another use for my knife.

Tiresias:

…look in the mirror and see yourself holding back like me
in that place of uncertainty
where you want to help but don't know when or how
in any case mirrors often play tricks so one minute
you'll exist and the next you're gone.

you can disappear like that from a life
be forced to vanish
to run away, be chased away
from everything you took for granted
you join a multitude of migrants all carrying a story
looking for somewhere safe
to set it down and build a life again

you walk a tightrope between hope and despair
memorising the uses of forgiveness
when someone shows you your face in the mirror
you don't recognise yourself
judged for your journey, suspected for your silence

this woman's story is a hall of mirrors with many versions
betrayal at the heart of all of them
if she sees how well I listen she may mark me
as her witness when we meet
between her lost voice and my blinded sight

Philomela

no tapestry in this version nor nightingale
no need for mercy from the gods
my sister spared the outcome of her rage
my nephew saved the violence of revenge
the only weaving is my story with others
truth another kind of vengeance
as I grow wings ready for flight.

A GIRL IN THE WOODS

I make myself clean in the forest,
I brush my arms over the ferns.
It's better when it rains and
the forest is sighing with damp.

It holds water like a sacrifice.
I give it blood. It holds blood.
The trees give me their silence,
always there, under the moon.

I walk in the forest until my lungs ache.
I walk fast, up bouldered paths. I lose
the way. It's better like that, losing
your way. No hope of being found.

There's nothing to lie in the dark
waiting for, biting your lip. Nothing
to wait for and want, so it's over and
done with. Nothing to be blamed for.

You don't have to be clean, or worry
how you look. You can get clean there.
You can lean against the bark of a tree
and make yourself clean. No-one sees.

Muddy girl in the woods, painting it red.
And leaves make good bandages.
You fix them like a bracelet. Fix them.
Fix everything. No-one ever needs to know.

VAGABONDA

THE GO-AWAY BIRD

Woken by the nasal *kweh, go-way* call
of the grey lourie bird, the descending
drawl of its last syllable, I remember
where I am. Dear bird with your wispy
swept-back crest, your long grey tail,
don't say *go-way*, *go-way*. I've been
too long away and hearing you is like
a door opening. Send a welcome down
from your feasting perch in the fig tree.
Please be kind and change your tune,
ask me to *stay awhile, stay awhile* –
long enough to hear your name again
in other tongues: Umklewu, Kwevoel,
learn to speak them without faltering.

THERE WILL NEVER BE ANOTHER

moment like this, time on my hands
out of the rain in a place called Extra Virgin

with Italian wedding soup on the menu
cappuccino and green orchids on the table

a basket of oranges ready for juicing
the hiss of the espresso machine

red blooms on the bar, the autumn colour
of a Virginia Creeper I once had.

Rain came at 4pm as predicted
they say this city never sleeps

my hands smell of cedar trees
no-one but me knows exactly where I am.

VAGABONDA

They were my travelling days of no-fixed abode
nowhere to call a home. My heartbreak years

filled with so much heart to heart, so many
open-hearted meetings. "Vagabonda", she said

the Italian poet I met in Egypt. "It's your name
for these times, these lush years of being open

on the move, a free spirit, wanderer, wayfarer
roamer, bird of passage, pilgrim meanderer.

underneath the peeling paint and shabby tiles
of South Kensington underground station
when you choose right to the Piccadilly Line
instead of left to District and Circle because
you think it might be quicker since there are
less stops and your feet turn you that way
but it's a long way further than you thought
even though the train is faster, and makes you
wonder how it would have been to choose
the other way, the way you'll never know, not even
when you get there, to St Pancras, looking back
to that moment, no matter how clearly you can see
the walls, the shabby tiles, that moment of indecision
then decision and you realise you'll never be able
to make that other particular journey on this day
at that particular moment, so when you sit drinking
cappuccino instead of latte in Carluccio's, you realise
you won't know that other journey the way you know
the taste of latte that once foamed hot on your lips.

of a dog, followed by another dog. The insistence of each crack
in the paved terrace and two women, still as the legs of the table.
Take a pool, take a coffee cup kicked over, take the need to wash

the stain out of a turquoise sandal, the sweep of it through water.
What happens to the shine, the bells breaking over a half-finished
wall, one red pomegranate amongst the green? A solitary ant

weaves a way back, makes a bridge of its body to cross the cracks.
A woman bites a pear. Its skin is the colour of another woman's skirt.
Filaments of red in the wind. The wood of a chair. A fistful of seconds.

SOME MIGHT CALL YOU DEADWOOD

but there's motion in your peeling bark risen
like a sail in the wind. A fresh cloverleaf

and some grey-green lichen are clinging on
as if they can't believe there's no hope now

and since you're giving off a hint of smoke
I'm wondering if you've suffered fire damage

and whether this fallen knot of bark curled
into itself could be a ship's wheel and the sail

become a rudder to help you steer your way
to the underworld with your leaf and lichen lovers?

I WANTED TO WRITE ABOUT FALLING

because I'd tripped as I hurried to catch
the bus to St Pancras from the Southbank
where I'd heard about Bertolt Brecht and
Greta Steffin falling (in love in their case),
and then had fallen on palms and knees, despite
which I made it to the train where I fell into
a conversation with a woman who looked
as if she might burst into tears, until I leaned
across the aisle with a question, discovered
she was en route to her dad's 80th birthday
but was afraid she'd have to turn back since
she'd lost her artist's toolbox, full of items
that were essential if she were to avoid falling
behind and missing an important deadline,
at which point I suggested she could phone
Carluccio's where she believed she'd left it,
ask them to keep it safe until the next day,
so she did, which just goes to show how
some things can sometimes fall into place.

CALVARY

The particular purple of an un-named flower
takes its place above the crown of my head.
A church bell rings somewhere no more specific
than *over there* which makes other bells reply,

as if the bells are all there is for a moment, drowning
out the voices and shuffle of feet. I look up to where,
they say, you arrive if you climb the Calvary steps,
follow the Stations of the Cross. There's a church

where I would have lit a candle, but for the fact it was
closed – for renovation. And yes, I still light candles
in Catholic churches, though I am no longer a believer.

A swallow turns the sun off and summer is in ruins,
like that summer on Ilkley Moor – rocks named after
beasts, me stalking them for ways through the impasse.

DISTRACTIONS

There's no obvious way to shift me from a life
of necessary solitude, though I sometimes

miss the joy of slipping from the warm side
of a sleeping lover to watch the moon

through cold curtains. Life is a stolen word
from someone else's lines, but can it harm

if it's surrounded by my own? In the nearest café,
I miss out main course, bite into blueberry sponge.

This is a city where cold applies mainly
to the weather, where people butter their bread

and remember which side. These inventions
of mood are not always useful and this may not be

the right place to say, but there's a woman
on the next table who keeps casting glances.

There's so much shame in her eyes and
all I can do is smile and watch her plumage

bristle under the beige of her fleece, thinking
"What's to lose? Take off the jacket and fly!"

EL GOUNA WRITERS' RESIDENCY

Coffee in the hotel lobby where I sink
into the plush russet velour of a sofa.
The clink of a cup as a woman pours
lemon tea from her teapot. The rain
has brought everyone indoors, except
for one woman under the canvas awning
reading a book with *Song* in the title,
still smoking her Marlborough Light.
Paintings of palm trees in ornate frames
and brass planters beside a carved door,
with yukkas looking worse for wear.
"Unseasonal rain" says the young man
mopping up under various verandahs
where the canopies have been leaking.
A jar on the shelf is full of what might be
red and yellow fruit or could be peppers
that look like a face with a glass veil.
At the piano a man sings *Surfin' USA,*
Sweet Little Sixteen, Pretty Woman.
I'm a poet alone in a hotel in Egypt
who could be anywhere in the world.

WHAT IT IS

It's the light. It's a woman hanging clothes
to dry on the rooftop of a half-finished building

beyond my roof terrace wall, like things planned,
like beginnings and patience enough to wait until

there's time and money for endings. It's the call
to prayer, then another call from another mosque

in the music of a language unknown yet familiar.
It's the repetition, like intercessions, like calling

to a god, like calling to belief and the whole valley
echoing with something more than the material

fact of my body sipping lemon tea, in the shade
with the sun throwing its light back at me.

RED

In my room everything is blue: the shutters, curtains, bedspread, the railings outside. Not to mention the sea and sky. They're fighting it out on the other side of my window in that place on the horizon where they seem to touch.

But this is not about blue. The red stripes in the paintings on the wall are here to remind me. So too the red nightshirt, which I never wear for sleeping but throw on each morning to shield me from the invasion of blue when I open my shutters.

You could say I am having an affair, though it has barely started. And now I have begun to speak of it in this way, it may lose its fascination. But for now I will behave as if I am already in the mesh. If I am honest it is the rekindling of an earlier passion.

Let me explain. I am on a bridge in Dublin. To be precise it is the Rory O'More Bridge over the River Liffey. The bridge is blue. My trousers are red. I am in love with the photographer. This is an old photograph.

Another photo. Not so old but just as red: shirt, necklace, earrings, my lips and a sunburned look that could pass for russet. I am still in love. It is, once again, with the photographer but a different one. She is backing away. I know this and pretend that I don't. Surprisingly, it doesn't affect the quality of the photograph or the sincerity of my smile.

I once lived in a house full of porcelain bowls. They were so delicate I was always afraid of collision. The bowls were mostly blue and white. My new house is filled with red Calla Lilies. They lean on my white walls like tired onlookers.

Thanks to Anne Carson I have an autobiography of red to refer to. It tells me that *desire is no light thing*. As if, of all people, I needed to be told! I know the weight, mass, length and breadth of it and still I am no nearer to understanding how it can so easily slip through your fingers.

There is a red flower on the mountain walk that looks as if it could be eaten, like fruit. However, it is possibly poisonous. Some days I think I am fine as I am, until a chance encounter makes me yearn for red. But everything is muted earth except for the woman at the next table. Her sun-kissed shoulders are draped with a scarf of scarlet leaves. They burn away all traces of betrayal.

NCEBA

When we meet, you are studying how stars circle round
each other, suck energy, move closer together until
they merge. Searching your laptop, your slender fingers

clicking at the keyboard, you're excited to show me pictures
of these binary stars, explain the details of a doppler effect.
You work in atomic time, and have no interest in the history

of clocks, as you wait for the imminent unveiling of the largest
optical telescope in the southern hemisphere with hexagonal
mirrors, measuring eleven metres wide, which will enable

spectroscopic and polarimetric analysis. The words mean little
to me but, as you speak, I'm held by your energy, its brightness
shining under your skin, intense as the pinpoint light of stars.

PLEASE DO NOT LITTER THE BEACH WITH…

Muizenberg, Cape Town

traces of footprints from the past.
Do not look up at the haze of distance
as you wrap a cinnamon scarf around
your shoulders. Please be as still as
the seagull on a rusted pole above you
and watch the curve of cormorants
or the shadow of a man's arm brushing
yellow paint on the beach hut's tongue
and groove. Please lie down and leave
an imprint: the pockets of your jeans,
your belt, that hollow like a broken wing
in the centre of your back. Please watch
small blobs of cloud, in an otherwise
cloudless sky. Up they go like a stairway.

FISH ON THE ROCKS

Hout Bay, Cape Town

The seagulls are after my hake
and who could blame them
for craving these soft flakes
of fish, the salty crisp of batter.
I eat the last morsels, drinking tea
with long-life milk as the sun sets
and clouds change shape. I can see
as far as the rocky end of the beach

where a child from the township
once drowned and though he ran,
risking the churning waves, Simon
was too late to save him. Beyond
a curve of limestone above the fynbos,
a single float hovers in the sea's swell.

A CAFÉ CALLED BEST UGLY

Seapoint, Cape Town

I walk along the promenade past joggers
of all shapes and sizes. A team of workers
collects ropes of seaweed against a wall.
Black women are pushing the wheelchairs
of their elderly white employers, giving them
sunshine and sea air or taking white babies
out for a walk. In the café, two white women
are complaining about their black employees
with such disrespect, such cold disregard.
What can I say about all this? The menu says
music's the only language everyone understands.
In Namaqualand, a day's drive away, spring flowers
are beginning their brief lives, transforming
the arid landscape with their lush orange beauty.

LEFTOVERS

Kalk Bay, Cape Town

There's a chain, beyond which I could stand
to watch the sea spilling over the harbour walls,
but a man who's fishing tells me to step back.
"You'll be drenched or, worse still, picked up
and tossed over by a wave." A seal snorts
at the water lapping on the steps behind me.
On the deck of a boat called *Alma Lucie*
pink leggings are hanging out to dry, albeit
in moist air. The day's catch has come and gone,
women are no longer gutting fish, there's no-one
sleeping under the arches. The last dregs of a day
and as the sun disappears behind the mountain
I find myself at an empty table in Kalky's fish bar
eating leftover calamari that needs more spice.

HARVESTING

Kalk Bay, Cape Town

At Olympia café's vineyard
in a place I call home for now
I'm filling a crate with dusty
purple clusters of Cabernet Franc,

though I may not be here
to drink the wine. Packed
tight to the vine, they resist
detachment and I slice my finger

as if it's a stalk, watch my blood
mingle with grape juice. Later
stripped bare, steeped in the loss

of grapes, the vineyard holds on
to the aroma. I'm left with stained
fingers and a cut that's slow to heal.

WILD SPIRIT LODGE

Tsitsikamma National Park

I wake up laughing, as the light arrives:
deep pink bands slowly bleach
to pastel, blend with blue.
There's hardly a breeze but a bush
nearby sways as if rocked by
an invisible hand. Trees sprout
on a ridge like tufts of hair
on a sleeping giant. The yellow-wood
tree is thirty metres high,
more than a thousand years old
and voices under her leaves
seduce me like a new lover,
whispering, "Stay, stay here,"
as eucalyptus and lavender tangle my feet.

AT THE SLAVE LODGE

Cape Town

She is the woman who, after disappearing in the curse
of a ship, finds herself newly arrived under the mountain.

They call her no name, then a new name in another language;
they write her name on page 472, Slave Lodge Census 1714.

Maria of Ceylon, counted, accounted for in the roll call,
in a pebbled courtyard where she counts stones,

digs at the dirt in cracks between the stones, marks hours
until the hour when the doors are opened for the pleasure

of free men. No, in any language, should be understood,
but she is the silenced goods and worth three inches of tobacco

to the man who's trading her. When men with strange voices
fall on her in turn, she is the woman with numbers rattling

behind her teeth – eka, deka, tuna, hatara, paha, haya, hata,
ata, navaya, dahaya – counting stones, counting shapes

in the red of her eyelids, who is unravelling threads of herself.
She pulls them out, lays them warp and weft, on the stone floor,

reweaves the fabric of her flesh. She is the woman who is waiting
for the rain, waiting for the Yala Monsoon to uproot her silence.

*Built in 1679 to house the slaves of the Dutch East India Company at the Cape. The doors of the Lodge were open to free men between eight and nine every evening, to be used as a brothel.

NAMING THE PAGES

"..judging by the large number of portraits in which they appear, many of the black pages could not have been more than nine or ten years old."
(*Staying Power*, Peter Fryer, p.72)

Many portraits of aristocrats in the 17th and 18th century include a black child. It was the 'fashion' at the time to have enslaved black children as servants. In effect this meant that children were bought, sold, renamed and moved from house to house. These "trafficked" children were included in portraits as representations of the aristocrat's wealth and status and rarely recognized as sitters in their own right. The tendency to marginalize them has largely persisted to this day, as evidenced most clearly by the fact that portrait titles seldom acknowledge their presence. Listen. The nameless "page" in Sudbury Hall will speak first, making way for more voices.

ALL THE CAPTIVE CHILDREN

If I'd been "handcuffed to history" like Rushdie's
midnight's children, instead of shackled to slavery,
if I'd inherited Saleem's gift and could summon
all the captive children, I would gather them here
in the drawing room of Sudbury Hall. Each of us,
hunted down by traders, transported by slave ships,
stripped of our family trees, has been immortalised
in oils, and hung unnamed in numerous stately halls.

I'd ask the boys at Petworth if they feel resentful
of the animals they pose with, since the Seymours
grant a higher status in their household to the dog
and horse than those who groom and care for them.
The girl at Belton House might disagree and tell us
how it comforts her to hold a lapdog on her knee,
while the boy at Sprivers with a silver tray of fruit
complains about its weight in his aching arms.

I'd want the boy from Claydon House (a souvenir
from Guineau, courtesy of the Royal African Company)
to let us know the name he had, before he was abducted
and named Peregrine by an uncle of Lord Verney.
This might move the boy from Saltram House
to tell us how the Admiral he stands beside is the man
who seized him, took his name, brought him as a trophy
on his ship, dressed him up and named him Jersey.

Each one of us would have the chance to speak
and listen: the barely visible page at Oxburgh Hall,
and the lost boy at Trerice House who are both
shadows of themselves; the child servant at Upton;
the boy with the Duke of Devonshire at Hardwick Hall;
two from Ham House in white silk and pearl earrings;
and the unnamed page at Seaton Delavel whose job
is to hold the arrows for the family's only son and heir.

I'd sit beside the boy from Montacute and discover
how the painter Vanderbank dressed us both in red,
made us hold the hem of a gown for hours, our necks
aching as we followed orders to gaze up at its wearer.
And I'd let the groom at Charlecote know how much
I envy the consolation of a horse nuzzling his head
and soothing the rising panic, as he strains like me
to breathe and swallow inside his metal collar.

IN WHICH THE CAPTIVE CHILDREN BEGIN TO SPEAK

The Hon. Anne Howard, Lady Yonge
(John Vanderbank, 1737)
Sudbury Hall

When they brought me here, the strange noises
that passed between them were like stones falling
on my head, until I learned to look for meanings.

My name is the one they use for the flimsy things
inside a binding they call leather. They say book
and their eyes look down on marks called words.

I match the sounds they make to things I see
and read their moods in the foreign language
of their faces. But I won't let my tongue curl

and speak them out. Silence is my hiding place.
I have the lock and key. I'll not open the door.
Some pages may offer words. This one is silent.

They place me at the edge of the portrait
like an afterthought, an aside, half-hidden
by the hem of a dress, which I must hold

at a particular height so the folds will catch
the light from the window. My neck aches
and the weight of her gown drags at my arms.

She has a boy of her own, I saw him running
past the shaped hedges down to the lake.
I am landlocked, padlocked in a silver collar

while in my head stories of home run amok
as if to taunt me: my mother's hand touching
my forehead, my bare feet pounding the earth.

Sir Thomas Lucy
(Godfrey Kneller, 1680)
Charlecote Park

Painted a darker shade than the horse I groom,
you might not see me standing in the right hand
corner of this work of art, were it not for the way

the artist has captured the light that is falling on
this silver collar squeezing my neck. Look for
the white in the horse's eye then follow its gaze

until you see the glint of metal that's fastened
so tight that it hurts each time I try to swallow.
Raise your eyes and you'll see the face of a boy

without a name, painted to be barely visible.
I am the groom. They call me blackamoor.
The horse nuzzles my head, her breath is warm.

John Delavel as an Archer, with a Black Page
(William Bell, 1770)
Seaton Delavel Hall

They say I belong to this boy of fourteen
younger than me and smaller, who calls himself
my master. You see that ornate bow he holds,

it's nothing but a prop. Those weak arms of his
have never readied an arrow to shoot, never felt
the force of a pulled bowstring, the heat of a kill.

My arms are strong enough to hold the weight
of these silver-tipped arrows. They are restless
like me, to be let loose and fly, to escape from

this towering ornate castle, and this boy
who thinks he owns me. This boy who looks,
for all his wealth, as if he won't reach twenty.

Mary Elizabeth Davenport with her page
(John Vanderbank, c1730)
Montacute House

Draw a line from the ochre urn on its plinth
down the curve of grey satin tied in the hair
of this pale woman and you'll see me staring

at the blue velvet of her sleeve, the white lace
of her cuff. These strange buckled shoes pinch
my toes and the red stockings make my legs itch.

I want to scratch but my fingers must hold still
and echo the shape of hers, though they ache
with the weight of her dress. I matter less to her

than the feather in her right hand. The artist
cares only for the powders he mixes with oil
to make the colours he daubs on the canvas.

Mary Lawley, 2nd wife of Sir John Verney
(Lenthall, c1694-1702)
Claydon House

There's fire in my belly, its heat prickles my skin.
Behind this smile they've painted on my face
rising bile makes me retch. I try to swallow

and the metal collar tightens. They gave me a name
which sits on my tongue like dust, no more mine than
this silk draped on my shoulder to catch the angle

of light, the way it catches the folds on her dress.
The captain who bought me for two yards of cloth
threw my own name overboard then stowed me

in his cabin as a souvenir with the rest of his cargo.
Hungry for the taste of fufu, I lay awake each night
listening to men and women wailing below decks.

Belton Conversation Piece
(Philip Mercier c 1726)
Belton House

The day they brought me here, a white powder
was falling from the sky. It landed on my hands
and face, then disappeared and left a chill.

I know their changing seasons now, the way
I've come to know my place. With less status
than the dog on her lap, I push the wheelchair

of the Viscount's invalid wife, dressed in brown
and gold to mirror her gown. She is heavy and
I'm hungry for comfort but no-one speaks to me.

Why look at the clouds? I'm a boy without wings,
no more than a shadow in their grand house
full of cold corridors and even colder hearts.

Mary Helden with her black page
(Charles Phillips, 1739)
Sprivers

The peach on this silver tray smells ripe enough to eat.
I think its juice might quench my thirst. I lean forward
on my right leg as if I'm about to walk out of this picture,

as if I could rip off these strange clothes, run to the fields
and eat until I'm full. The painter snaps orders at me:
as he strokes the dog, 'Hold still, you're dreaming again,

lift the tray higher, turn your head, let your gaze rest
on her pink cheeks.' I stare past her to the red curtain
that is like a cloud of fire. I can dream in the day but

at night, knees pulled up to my chest, I wrap myself
around my empty feelings. I crave touch but no-one
ever lays a hand on me: not in anger or with kindness.

SITTING FOR THE MISTRESS

Portrait of Louise Keroualle, Duchess of Portsmouth, Mistress of Charles II, posing with her black child servant (detail)
Pierre Mignard, 1682

First sitting
Blackbird lives inside me – the mistress knows.
She calls me her *petite merlette*, tells me
I mustn't worry because inside my black skin
is a soul as white as the pearls she has tied
so tight around my neck. She says I was three
when she washed the devil away and if I do
bad things she'll have to clip my blackbird wings.
The mistress says I must stand beside her while
Monsieur Mignard makes us up with colours,
that we will be a painting in a gilded frame,
hanging in the halls of the Palace of Whitehall,
her skin lead-white against the lamp-black of mine.
My head begins to spin and Monsieur shouts,
Tilt your chin up! Look at the mistress, not me!

Second sitting
There are feathers everywhere. I sweep them
into small piles far down below my ribs
and smile like the mistress tells me. She has
a face like stone that never smiles. Parched lips
stretch out across dry teeth and pull my cheeks.
The face very close in my dream was squeezing mine
as if our cheeks would melt, tears trickling over me
and the mouth kissing. Blackbird starts to tremble
and then the feathers blow: they clog my throat.
When I cough them out the mistress laughing
says I bark like one of the King's spaniels,
Merlette aboye comme une chien! I count
the clouds still drifting in a painted sky
behind her head till blackbird falls asleep.

Third sitting
Blackbird sleeps while Monsieur Mignard mixes
colours in his pots of clay. My hand's
too small to hold this shell that's full of pearls.
If I shake, the shell tips up and the pearls fall,
the mistress will be angry. One red jewel,
two red jewels, three – drip from her dress.
Blackbird rouses. The mistress rests her arm
across my back, so light a touch, a tickle
on my shoulder. A touch, a lift, strong arm
round my legs, a hand cupped in my armpit,
fingers pressing my back. Blackbird flutters.
Heavy eyes count her back to sleep. One red
jewel, two red – Mistress nips my shoulder.
Look at me and smile, Merlette! You'll spoil the picture!

Fourth sitting
Blackbird is learning to be still, she watches
Monsieur Mignard as he watches me. The mistress
has blue sleeves that drape like open curtains,
the swirls on her golden dress are falling leaves.
The coral chafes my fingers, rough as the blanket
we hide under in the damp room that smells
of the big grey water. At night I push my fist
into my mouth, bite my knuckles till I see
maman. She's an obechi tree. I claw
at her, my leg reaching to find a foothold
but she's being dragged away smaller and smaller
and then she disappears. Blackbird wails,
her wings screaming at the criss-cross window.
She thuds down. I suck in breath, stay very still.

Fifth sitting
Blackbird wants to teach me how to fly
over the palace gardens. There are bitter
berries hidden in the swish of leaves
beside the golden sundial that the mistress
calls *les mures de ronce* – she rolls the words
like pearls on her tongue. She sits on her velvet stool
and tells me I must be *comme une statue.*
Blackbird pecks my inside skin so my legs
begin to shake. She spreads her wings, pushes
at my ribcage, whirls into the sky screeching.
I want to stop my ears but my hands are full,
my cheeks sting, and I can't find Blackbird
until I hear her call Maman, Maman!
You've no Maman, I cry, you're much too wicked.

AFTER-WORDS

ARE YOU WRITING?

I would write but one side of the page
keeps slipping below the water level.
Diving's not my thing, or I'd practice
going under and anyway doesn't paper
have a tendency to float? I see it rising
to the surface, but alas too near
to the propellers of my boat to risk
me hanging over for a safe retrieval.

These days only clay makes sense,
my fingers, sticky with the substance of it,
try to feel their way back to something –
once my habit. It's been wearing thin.
I make vessels that become more fragile
as they dry. They need fire for strength.

GHAZAL: HEARTSEASE

Words scramble out of reach, caught in the sycamore trees
on the rambling rose, but this garden brings its heartsease.

Your quiet presence in the red and ochre of my present
soothes me like a tulip's promise of Spring's heartsease.

You grew blueberries for my pleasure, made an arch
curved like wings where my clematis clings with heartsease.

The roses were always for you, now they grace the life we share.
Look, the lush profusion of the Poet's Wife sings its heartsease.

And now this poet, watching my beloved's hands work wood,
recalls the gold of oak and beech on wedding rings: its heartsease.

SEA POOLS

Salt water left from the last tide,
like tears from the last shedding.
I spread my arms as if they could
be wings and walk towards
the red glow under the surface
but it's only a pebble stained by
an encounter. This is a story
of someone, perhaps me, looking
for a way to say 'sadness'
like the intermittent sound
of notes blown into the wind
becoming silence. And still
no tears. Say one pool then
another. Stand between them.

REFLECTIONS

i.m Teresa Seneviratne 1948-2020

I wander in woodland where cattle wait in line
to rub their black hides against a fissured alder.
A yew's bark peels open, the page of an unread book
that untethers me from all my scattered elsewheres.
The sturdy bulk of a cedar of Lebanon beckons me,
one branch low enough to wrap my arms around.
I let it lift my feet, take my weight, rock my sorrows,
secure me to the solid presence of this day.

*

Because I can't be at her funeral, I make an altar
in my living room: an oak table with indigo shawl,
a lit candle on a birch holder with a heart in its bark.
I gather camellias – the petals fall, the way she fell
quietly away after all the sorrow of the incremental
losing of her, all the living with her present absence.
I send my love out to their broken heartache, a circle
of held hands around the space she has left.

*

Two yellow iris petals, purple-veined, stamens
still reaching towards the light, have fallen.
My fingers cradle them like an arm would
a sleeping baby as I float them, let them loop
their skirts over the edge of a shallow dish.
Bleached, translucent, they curl like embryos
around themselves in the violet water, until
they are reminiscent of the buds they came from.

*

The longest day brings the gift of an evening drive
to Longdale, where we lie on lush green between
the lines of trees, waiting for owls that never come.
A song thrush serenades us and it feels like the sun
will never set; still light enough to walk over the hill
down to the grassy path that curves beside a cattle field.
On the way back I am that child, body full of outdoors,
wrapped up against the chill, being driven home to bed.

*

Rain wakes me, loud against the felted covering
above my head. Instead of sheep, I count
birch slats that gather towards the roof ring
at the apex of this yurt (our temporary dwelling)
with thoughts of my agapanthus, blooming unseen
in our garden, recalling how the light through
the burnished red of the acer had dispelled
all my uncertainties before we left home.

*

Ducks, wings, a daughter and the mothering of her –
such dreams one night that I chuckle in my sleep.
She's all ages and no particular age, snug with me
on a pocket of land so small, so edged up to the water
that ducks are bumping into us as they glide past.
One is curious, nudges her, then lifts its wings,
lets the wind carry it low over the water. We watch
marvelling at the way a body can be lifted in flight.

*

'I'm happy here', I say. Meaning not happy as such but
happy to stay while Billie sketches the outline of a rock.
My body is unsettled despite the sun across the water,
the view down the coast to our lighthouse cottage,
the water always breaking in a gentle way against rocks
that sometimes look like seals. I see one lift its head
with sad eyes and a whiskery face, so I call it a sea rabbit,
then hold its gaze until my body finds its own stillness.

*

I wouldn't say she collects empty nests, it's more like
they arrive, they find her somehow. To house them
she has built a nature box that hangs in the porch.
They are homes beside the door to our home.
They are safe places, green, white, brown and black
held together with mud and the silk of cobwebs.
If they could speak they would say, we are here
to remind you of the resilience of fragile things.

ROCK-A-BYE BABY TREE

It's like walking in a lush wood and entering
a clearing where felled trees make the landscape

look dystopian, but you walk through it anyway
because you're looking for the ancient yew tree –

the one they call the rock-a-bye baby tree –
and when you find it burnt out, you go up close

to hold it, which is how you discover the way the bark
has kept its beauty in the fire and there's a hollow

that looks like a cradle and you almost miss it –
the two-leafed beginnings of another yew.

BESIDE THE MULBERRY TREE

i.m. Chris Bilson 1949-2012

When we first met, your sister told me
how she'd lost you in that Cretan autumn,
summer heat still lying heavy on the land.
Through love and law you would have been
my brother. You share my father's name,
now I share her loss of you. How is it possible
that I miss you though we've never met?

You lived and worked at Plakias youth hostel
where you coaxed branches of mulberry trees
to intertwine across a path of stone circles.
I want to lean my back against the trunk
of this young mulberry planted in memoriam
but twenty-seven snails cling to its bark
hovering between motion and stillness.

I wish I'd had the chance to hear the shifting
tones of your voice recounting your story
of arriving here, or to tell you how I love
the wild white iris flourishing by the road,
how I saw my first swallowtail butterfly
or to ask you if forests of false fennel have
always competed with olive trees for height.

I wasn't there when she buried your body
in the only foreigner's grave at Myrthios
but five years later another foreigner died
and I heard her make the call to Fr. Antonios
giving him permission to disinter your bones,
wash them in wine, place them in a metal chest
according to the customs of Greek Orthodoxy.

We find your ossuary in the cemetery chapel
at Myrthios, where she unpacks each bone,
stained russet-red 'and lighter than you'd think',
she says, handing me your thigh bone so I can feel
its weight. She strokes remnants of hair still soft
on your skull. Meeting not flesh but substance,
material being, I'm as close as I'll ever be to you.

LETTER TO ANNA AKHMATOVA

Dear Anna

Reading your poem about Dante has taken me back
to meeting him, after climbing to the highest point
above the highest of the Bagni di Lucca villages.

Head and shoulders cast in bronze, his stern face
looked towards the cemetery's elaborate mausoleums,
with their framed photographs of the departed.

I was haunted by my own trail of deaths and longing for
another generation to be born: children who could listen
to my stories of ancestors they'd never met.

There was an epic family saga I had always meant to write:
losses and leavings, sea crossings between Asia and Europe
and a mother who might begin the story.

There is so little I know of her, yet that day she seemed
to share her thoughts with me, her body heavy with worry
for the child who would become my grandfather.

It was as if she sensed how grief would send him off the rails
until a journey overseas that led him to a second wife –
although he'd never love her like the first.

I am telling you this because I think you will understand
what happened to me under the monument to Dante
as a kind of enchantment:

one that makes you doubt all notions of linear time
because when you go round in circles, it's possible
to be both behind and ahead of time.

I'd like to have met you, even though I never got beyond
making footprints on Moscow airport's snowbound runway
as I made my way to the transit lounge.

Anyway it would have been impossible then, because
you were almost five years dead and I couldn't stop
since I was on my way, for the first time,

to see Sri Lanka, the place of my grandfather's birth,
which was, as it happens, in the same year as yours,
albeit continents apart.

All of which leaves me some hope of a meeting point
on our respective circles, where you'll reach out to me
ahead of your time as I reach back from mine.

ONE HUNDRED WORDS FOR LOVE

i.m. Tony Seneviratne 1928-2023

Because you were my favourite uncle
who helped me hold onto my mother
at my father's funeral, to stop her falling
into his grave during the incessant prayers
of the presiding priest. Because you wrote
my name in Sinhala script after a man
in Avisawella, who looked like family,
sent us to Rakwana, where a priest named
Charles de Gaulle promised to search
the baptism records for our ancestors.
Because of the stories over sundowners
watching the swallows skim the surface
of your pool in Akyaka. Because you always said,
"Why use one word when you can use a hundred?"

THE AGE OF REASON

For Annie

On a run-down station platform, after a trip to the gallery,
we discuss art and artists, which way the train might arrive.

Later at a Thai restaurant, you tell me you prefer eating food
from other parts of the world – India, Thailand, China, Italy,

tell me you are planning to live in a log cabin far from the city
when you grow up and you'll be as self-sufficient as you can

so you won't need much money. We discuss the difficulties
of living off the grid – storing ice-cream without a fridge.

You are seven years old making plans about your future
telling me you might break laws but only if they're bad ones.

Your wise questions 'Are there any laws you don't agree with?'
prompt me to talk about refugees, the laws that keep them out,

about your great granddad, who you never met, his arrival
all those years ago and the line of our unique family

through four generations, linking continents and cultures,
arriving here, to savour this food, this talk, this moment.

THE INDIAN PRINCE

For Lily

Because you are turning twelve today
I want to tell you about the Indian prince
we made when you were two.

You were a sad-eyed princess telling me
you had no prince to marry. 'Don't worry'
I said, gathering three cushions to hand.

His top embroidered with an elephant,
his pants adorned with birds and flowers
enclosed in gold-edged squares.

Lemon eyes, satsuma nose, the curve
of a banana smile on the bright red
mirrored cushion of his head.

His legs were Kenyan salad servers carved
from olive wood. Two spoons for arms –
one Sri Lankan coconut, another English pine.

In the absence of a crown, a plastic bowler hat
worked well and for Princess Lily's cloak
a cloth with marching elephants.

A photo-shoot was vital, you were suitably serene
but the prince kept misbehaving, losing legs
and messing up his clothes.

I scolded, 'Stop distracting us' and with a giggle
you gathered up the word, *distracting,* like a gift
to wrap your tongue around.

What times we had, Lily, replaying that script
word for word, for weeks on end, recreating
every detail of the made-up prince!

When you left, I'd tidy up the day's make-believe,
the sparkle of your voice still bright in the room
'Say it again, grandma, say it again!'

ACKNOWLEDGEMENTS

Grateful acknowledgement is made to the editors of the following journals and anthologies where some of these poems or versions of them appeared:

100 Queer Poems (Penguin Random House 2022); *Her Wings of Glass* (Second light Publications 2014); *Ten Anthology* (Bloodaxe 2010); *Siècle 21* (2012); *Rialto 91, Rialto 96* (2018 & 2021).

Thanks as ever to Mimi Khalvati my friend and mentor for her insightful feedback, continued love and support. To Jeremy Poynting and Hannah Bannister at Peepal Tree Press for their encouragement and commitment to editing and publishing my work. To Chloe for shared writing time. And of course to Billie, Kate, Simon Annie, Lily and all my family and friends, with gratitude for the numerous ways they enrich my life.

ABOUT THE AUTHOR

Seni Seneviratne, born and raised in Leeds, is of English and Sri Lankan heritage. She has given readings, performances and workshops in UK, US, Canada, South Africa, Egypt and Kuwait. She currently works as a freelance writer, mentor, trainer and creative consultant. Her poem 'A Wider View' is included on the AQA GCSE poetry syllabus.

Published by Peepal Tree Press, her debut collection, *Wild Cinnamon and Winter Skin* (2007), includes a poem, which was Highly Commended in the Forward Poetry Prize. *The Heart of It* (2012), her second collection, includes her poem 'Operation Cast Lead' which was shortlisted in the Arvon International Poetry Competition (2010). Her third collection *Unknown Soldier* (2019) was a PBS Recommendation, National Poetry Day Choice and highly commended in Forward Poetry Prizes 2020.

She is widely published in anthologies and magazines, most recently: *100 Queer Poems* (Penguin), *Where We Find Ourselves* (Arachne Press) *Wretched Strangers* (Boiler House Press), *The Rialto* and *New England Review*. She collaborates with film-makers, visual artists, musicians and digital artists, is one of ten commissioned writers on the Colonial Countryside Project (a child-led writing and history project with the University of Leicester, Peepal Tree Press and the National Trust) and is a fellow of the Complete Works programme for diversity and quality in British Poetry.

She has organised creative events and facilitated creative writing workshops and residences in schools, colleges and community settings, working across a range of abilities (from people with basic literacy skills to MA students) and with people from a variety of experiences and backgrounds. She is particularly interested in the relationship between poetry and trauma and has presented her paper, *Speaking the Unspeakable through Poetry: The Search for a Place of Healing and Witness after Trauma* at conferences in UK, US, South Africa and Kuwait.

In 2012 she was the poet in residence at the Ilkley Literature Festival and in 2013 she was commissioned by Aldeburgh Poetry

Festival to create text in response Bill Jackson's photographic exhibition, *Dark Light.* In 2014 her film-poem, 'Sitting for the Mistress' was shortlisted in the Southbank Film Poem competition. In 2016 she received an Arts Council grant to fund a collaboration with digital artist Shirley Harris to create a multi-media production, *Lady of Situations*, which was launched at Off the Shelf Literature Festival 2016.

She co-edited, *Out of Sri Lanka* – an anthology of Tamil, Sinhala and English poetry (Bloodaxe, June 2023) with Vidyan Ravinthiran and Shash Trevett. The book has received a PBS Special Commendation. She is currently working on an Arts Council Funded touring project based on her book, *Unknown Soldier* and an LGBTQ project with Sheffield Museums entitled *Queering the Archive.*

ALSO BY SENI SENEVIRATNE

Wild Cinnamon and Winter Skin
ISBN: 9781845230500; pp. 64; pub. 2007; £7.99

'Memory, from Yorkshire to Sri Lanka and back, Seni Seneviratne's poems delve in and out of a complex history. These tender, moving poems weave a delicate web.' — Jackie Kay

'There's something about us. There are historians that may record our experiences. And these experiences may be found in the galleries of the future. Preserved. But it's in the poetry where the exhibits actually live. And it's here. Let Seni walk you through the labarynthine gallery of wild cinnamon and winter skin.' — Lemn Sissay

'Seni Seneviratne's poetry straddles continents and centuries, and does so with an easy fluency. The reader is drawn into her journey of discovery for her 'cinnamon roots' and her exploration of issues of identity and relationships. Personal and universal histories interweave in these poems.' — Debjani Chatterjee

The Heart of It
ISBN: 9781845231903; pp. 64; pub. 2012; £8.99

'Here is a poet able to combine the personal in enchanting lyrics of desire with the political in poems that, through imaginative power, portray other lives – marginalised, brutalised, lost – as genuinely as her own. Seni speaks to us in a voice always natural, engaging, never pushing beyond the limits of authentic feeling but staying true to lived experience and, despite loss or heartache, always open to the outside world and its windows on the heart. *The Heart of It* is a tender, moving collection, full of passionate intensity and an unswerving faith in the power of reconciliation and love.' — Mimi Kalvati

Unknown Soldier
ISBN: 9781845234515; pp. 80; pub. 2019; £9.99

May 1941. Two signalmen meet for the first time in an army camp in the North African desert. The only surviving record of the friendship is an album of black and white photographs. The subject of the photographs is the first soldier, a twenty-four year old Ceylonese telephone and telegraph fitter who in 1940 enlisted in the Royal Signals. The second soldier is the photographer. This is the starting point for Seni Seneviratne's third collection. Through the photographs she finds the voices of the two men and thus begins her journey to meet her father, the first soldier, the unknown soldier.

Speaking in both in the voice of the father and of the unknown photographer, poems explore the mix of male camaraderie and casual racism of that experience, but also the deep affection hinted at in the way the photographer has framed "Snowball" in his lens. From this imaginative core, poems move out to make connections with the remembered and known life of a father who died too soon, to self-reflections on the poet as remembrancer, creator and actor in the world. There are moving poems on the meaning of inherited objects – a paper-knife, letters – and inherited ways of being – the birdwatching that provides a rich source of imagery. The personal moves out to the resonances of what was, in its origins, a story of migration. Here the father's success in finding of a home in Yorkshire is seen to contrast sharply with the tragedies of migrant deaths in the face of fortress Europe.

This is a work of great beauty, whose lucid simplicity of language is married to a rich complexity of structure and the bird-flight of images that connect poem to poem. There is humour, too, in the revenant voice of the mother who inserts herself into the poet's memory and demands in her "broad Yorkshire vowels [...] 'Why is your dad getting all the attention?'"